The World's Deadliest MAN-MADE DISASTERS

Claire Henry

PowerKiDS
press

New York

Published in 2014 by The Rosen Publishing Group, Inc.
29 East 21st Street, New York, NY 10010

First Edition

Produced for Rosen by Cyan Candy, LLC
Editor: Joshua Shadowens
Designer: Erica Clendening, Cyan Candy

Photo Credits: Cover Anthony Correia/Shutterstock.com; p. 4 arindambanerjee / Shutterstock.
com; pp. 5, 11, 14, 15, 16, 18, 19, 23 Shutterstock.com; p. 8 Kekyalyaynen / Shutterstock.com; pp.
9, 17, 21, 25 Photo by DAVID ILIFF. License: CC-BY-SA 3.0, via Wikimedia Commons; p. 10 (both)
Tim Dowd, via Wikimedia Commons, p. 12 Felix König, via Wikimedia Commons; p. 13 rijans,
via Wikimedia Common; p. 20 Samuel Acosta / Shutterstock.com; p. 22 Lindsaybridge, via
Wikimedia Commons; p. 24 Dan Howell / Shutterstock.com; p. 26 http://www.reyndar.org, via
Wikimedia Commons; p. 30 ChameleonsEye / Shutterstock.com.

Publisher Cataloging Data

Henry, Claire.
The world's deadliest man-made disasters / by Claire Henry — first edition.
  p. cm. — (The world's deadliest)
Includes index.
ISBN 978-1-4777-6144-1 (library binding) — ISBN 978-1-4777-6141-0 (pbk.) —
 ISBN 978-1-4777-6145-8 (6-pack)
1. Disasters — Juvenile literature. 2. Environmental disasters — Juvenile literature. I. Henry,
Claire, 1975–. II. Title.
D24.H46 2014
904—d23

Manufactured in the United States of America

CPSIA Compliance Information: Batch #W14PK8: For Further Information contact Rosen Publishing, New York, New York at 1-800-237-9932

TABLE OF CONTENTS

UNCOVERING MAN-MADE DISASTERS

In the 1970s, something strange began happening in the neighborhood of Love Canal, in Niagara Falls, New York. Plants were dying. Babies were born with health problems. Kids went out to play and came home with burns on their skin. The people of Love Canal soon found out they were living on 21,000 tons (19,051 t) of buried toxic waste that had begun to seep to the surface.

What happened in Love Canal is considered one of the worst man-made disasters in US history. Unlike natural disasters such as

CAR BOMB

Acts of terrorism in which many people are killed or injured are considered man-made disasters. Some police offices have the job of preventing terrorist attacks before they happen.

earthquakes and tornadoes, which are caused by nature, man-made disasters are caused by the actions of people. They include events such as oil spills, nuclear accidents, and plane crashes. In some cases, the full effects of a man-made disaster will not show up for many years!

Man-made disasters can injure and kill people, animals, and plants. They can also damage or destroy Earth's natural features, such as forests, lakes, and oceans.

In this book, you will read about some of the worst man-made

DEADLIEST MAN-MADE

NAME	DATE
September 11 Attacks	September 11, 2001
Texas City Disaster	April 16, 1947
Deepwater Horizon Oil Spill	April 20, 2010
Libby Asbestos Contamination	1919–1990
Oklahoma City Bombing	April 19, 1995
Donora Smog	October 27–31, 1948
Picher, Oklahoma Lead Contamination	1913–2009

disasters in history. You will find that some were caused because people did not understand the danger of their actions. In other cases, though, people ignored the danger and many others suffered as a result.

DISASTERS IN US HISTORY

LOCATION	DEATHS/DAMAGE
New York, Washington D.C., Pennsylvania	2,997+
Texas City, Texas	581+
Gulf of Mexico	11 dead, major damage to marine life
Libby, Montana	200+
Oklahoma City, Oklahoma	168
Donora, Pennsylvania	20 dead, 7,000 sick
Picher, Oklahoma	34% of children suffered from lead poisoning

POLLUTION AND TOXIC WASTE: POISONING EARTH

Man-made waste, or **pollution**, can be very dangerous for the environment. Garbage thrown into the ocean can kill birds and sea creatures. Smoke and harmful gasses released into the air cause **climate change** and warm the Earth. This can affect the habitats of many plants and animals, such as polar bears.

△ *Above*: Pollution sits over the city of Los Angeles.

◁ *Left*: The electricity plant seen here, in Russia, is causing air pollution.

Sometimes, pollution can become dangerous, and even deadly, to humans, too. Air pollution can make it hard for people to breath and cause illnesses such as asthma. When dangerous **chemicals** are buried in the ground or released into the air, they can contaminate drinking water and make people very sick.

DONORA SMOG

In October 1948, zinc and steel mills in the town of Donora, Pennsylvania, sent poisonous gases into the air, killing 20 people and making about 7,000 more sick. The Donora **Smog** is the worst air pollution disaster in US history.

PICHER, OKLAHOMA

The town of Picher, Oklahoma, was once a center of lead and zinc mining. However, waste materials left over from mining turned the area into one of the most toxic place in the United States, and it is now a ghost town.

These photos show the town of Picher, Oklahoma. On the right, you can see how close the piles of mining waste sat to homes.

NAMATA DISEASE

n the 1950s and 1960s, mercury, a toxic metal, was released as ste into Japan's Minamata Bay. The mercury contaminated the and shellfish in the bay, which were then eaten by the people of amata. At least 1,700 deaths occurred, though the actual number kely much higher.

London is famous for its fog. During the first days of the London Smog, most people did not realize that the thick smog was anything out of the ordinary.

LONDON'S GREAT SMOG

From December 5–9, 1952, London was covered with a thick yellow-black fog, called smog. The smog was caused by vehicle exhaust and the coal that many people burned to keep warm. When the smog lifted, at least 4,000 people had died, though the number could be closer to 12,000.

NUCLEAR MELTDOWNS AND INDUSTRIAL ACCIDENTS

Nuclear power can be a clean and safe way to produce energy. There are over 400 nuclear reactors in use around the world, producing 14% of the world's electricity. However, when something does go wrong at a nuclear power plant, it can send dangerous radiation into the surrounding area, affecting people and nature for years to come.

An accident at a nuclear plant is very dangerous. However, accidents can happen at other production plants and factories as well. These industrial accidents can be caused by dangerous materials being used inside the buildings. They can also be caused by unsafe working conditions.

NUCLEAR POWER PLANT

FACTORY COLLAPSE

On April 24, 2013, an eight-story building collapsed in Savar, Bangladesh. The people inside the building were mostly poor garment workers, sewing clothes to be sold in other countries. The factory had been built on swampy ground and with low-quality materials. At least 1,127 people were killed in the collapse.

CHERNOBYL NUCLEAR DISASTER

On April 26, 1986, an explosion at the Chernobyl nuclear power plant, in Ukraine, sent large amounts of **radiation** across Russia, Belarus, and other parts of Europe. The Chernobyl disaster's official death toll is 31 people, though thousands more suffered from birth defects and cancers.

WEST FERTILIZER COMPANY EXPLOSION

On April 17, 2013, a fire broke out at the West Fertilizer Company, in west Texas. As firefighters tired to put out the fire, the dangerous chemicals inside the building caused a large explosion. Fifteen people were killed and 160 were injured.

ABANDONED SCHOOL IN CHERNOBYL

The town of Pripyat was built to house the workers of the Chernobyl power plant and their families. Pripyat was abandoned after the Chernobyl disaster and is now called the "Lost City."

FUKUSHIMA DAIICHI NUCLEAR DISASTER

On March 11, 2011, water flooded and damaged the Fukushima Daiichi nuclear power plant in Japan. Scientists believe people living in the area were not exposed to enough radiation to cause health problems. However, it may be years before we know the actual effects of this disaster.

OIL SPILLS: DANGEROUS SLICKS

Crude oil, or petroleum, is a kind of fossil fuel. It formed from the remains of animals and plants that lived millions of years ago and are now buried under the ground. Oil is often used for heating. It is also used to make the gasoline that powers cars, buses, and planes.

Oil can be found under dry land or under bodies of water. It is taken from the ground using large drills and sent all around the world. Sometimes, though, large amounts of oil can spill into the environment. Oil spills damage ocean habitats and can kill animals.

SWAN

When oil gets on a seabird's feathers, they are no longer waterproof. The bird may get too cold or too hot. It may also try to clean its feathers and swallow dangerous amounts of oil.

This satellite photo shows the extent of the Gulf oil spill off the coast of Mississippi. The oil in the water reflects the Sun's light, making it appear bright.

DEEPWATER HORIZON

On April 20, 2010, an explosion on *Deepwater Horizon*, a floating oil rig in the Gulf of Mexico, killed 11 people. As the rig sank, millions of gallons (l) of oil gushed into the Gulf. The oil killed marine animals, such as dolphins, and made many animals very sick.

EXXON VALDEZ

The *Exxon Valdez* was a ship called an oil tanker. On March 24, 1989, the ship struck a reef in Alaska. Eleven million gallons (42 million l) of crude oil spilled into the ocean. Over 100,000 birds were killed, along with many otters, seals, and whales. Almost 25 years later, the area has not yet fully recovered.

GULF WAR OIL SPILL

On January 21, 1991, oil began pouring into the Persian Gulf, near the country of Kuwait. The oil spread out over 100 miles (160 km). The oil damaged salt marshes and other natural habitats.

This photo shows the effect of the *Deepwater Horizon* oil spill on a beach in Gulf Shores, Alabama.

ATLANTIC EMPRESS

In 1979, two large oil tankers collided in the Caribbean Sea. One of the ships, the *Atlantic Empress*, exploded. Twenty-six people were killed, and over 88 million gallons (333 million l) of crude oil spilled into the sea.

PLANE CRASHES AND MARITIME DISASTERS

Many people have a fear of flying. However, airplanes are actually one of the safest ways to travel. Accidents can happen, though. They are often caused by bad weather, engine failures, and bird strikes. In the United States, there are some years when hundreds of people die in plane crashes. In other years there are no deadly crashes.

Disasters can happen on the water, too. Before plane travel became common, people traveled across oceans in large ships, which sometimes sank. Today, people still use boats, such as ferries and cruise ships, to travel long and short distances.

IN MEMORY OF THOSE WHO PERISHED ON VALUJET FLIGHT 592 MAY 11 1996

JAMES EGBERT ALLAWAY
SAEEDA ALLIHASSEN
ISABEL BATISTA ANDERSON
LESLIE CAROL ARCHIBALD
MIAN RIZWAN ARSHAD
GIUSEPPE BAFUNNO
SEAN D. BAKER
THOMAS EUGENE BALANDRAN
MARLO AN CUEVAS BALANDRAN
JENNIFER ANN BARREIRO
HERBERT DUFFY BELL
PEGGY DWYER BELL
TERRI BELL
LEON ANTHONY BROWN
LYNN CECIL BROWN
FRANCES JACQUELINE BROWN
JOSEPH ARTHUR BURNETT
CECILIA CABRERA BAEZ
LISA MARIE CARLETON
RONNIE DUANE CARPENTER
SUSAN A WESTHOFF CARPENTER
NINON CORNEILLE
EDNA CRYE
KENNETH WOOD CRYE
KAREN DONNELLY CULVER
RODNEY DWAYNE CULVER
LORI MARIE CUSHING
DANIEL DARBOR
MANSOOR DARBOR
BRADLEY STEWART EHRLICHMAN
ELIZABETH THOMAS FAVERO
FRANCO FAVERO
LAURA ELIZABETH FAVERO
CHARLES JERRY FLUITT SR
PAMELA JEAN GABR
DEANA YEHIA GABR

ELIZABETH BENFIELD GABRIEL
CARLOS JESUS GONZALEZ BURGO
LILA VIOLETA VIZCAYA GONZALEZ
ANGELINE GREENE
MARK STEPHEN GRINER
STEPHEN KARL GULER
ANNA LAURIE HAMILTON
FELIX CONWAY HAMLTON
CAROL JUNE HANCHEY
JOHN TRAVIS HANCHEY
ELAINE L HAYMAN
ROBERT L HAYMAN
RICHARD SHERRILL HAZEN
WALTER HALE HYATT
DANNY CHARLES JARVIS
LINDA PASCHALL JARVIS
KATHLEEN JANE KESSLER
I SON KIM
CANDALYN CHAMBERLIN KUBECK
RAFAEL ANTONIO LAMEDA
ALIYAGI SHANTI LANDRY
DANNA LYN NELSON LANE
ROGER DAVID LANE
RAY WARREN LATHEM III
ANDREW CARL LEONARD
JEREMY R LEONARD
TABITHA RAE LEONARD
JIMMIE ALFRED LEWIS
DEVLIN LOUGHNEY
ROGER E LOUGHNEY
PHILMORE DELAND MARKS
BETTY MCLEMORE
CLARK BARTLEY MCNITT
JUDY MAIRE MCNITT
LAURA KATHRYN MCNITT
LINDSEY MILLER MCNITT
NEIL BARRY MCNITT

ROBERT FRANCIS MEDEIROS
JUDY ANN MEDEIROS
ELLA MARIE MITCHELL
ANDREW DAVID NEVIL
LUCILLE SUSCHE NEWBOLD
MAXWELL LEONARD NEWBOLD
WHILHELMENIA OLIVER
LISA PATREACE PEARSON
LAURESE ELIZABETH PERKINS
DAVID NEFTALY QUINONES
ELIDA VILMA RAMIREZ
KIMBERLY LYNNE RENNOLDS
DONNA LEE RENNOLDS
HOWARD LEE RIETZ
TERRI LYNN RUGG
DENNIS JULIUS SABO SR
ANA MARIA SANCHEZ
KARIN VALERIE SHIER
VIIOLA KARIN SHIER
JARVIS WAYNE SHOTWELL
RILVEN JOE SHOTWELL
JOYCE RILLA SIMONTON
PAUL JORDAN SMITH III
JOELAUR DONTE SNOWDEN
LOUISE WOOD STANLEY
HUGH WRIGHT STANLEY III
JENNIFER LYNN STEARNS
FRED JAMES STEINBRENNER JR
AMANDA LEIGH SUMMERS
JERROLD AUSTEN THOMPSON
ROOSEVELT TILLMAN
DELMARIE WALKER
JANICE JANE WEIMER
JAMES RICHARD WEIMER
TERESA KIM WILSON
RUTH MATTIE WOLFE
ROBERT WOODUS JR

This memorial lists the names of the 110 people who died in a plane crash in the Florida Everglades in 1996.

RMS TITANIC

The 1912 sinking of the *Titanic* is probably the most famous maritime disaster in history. The massive ship hit an iceberg in the Atlantic Ocean and 1,502 people were killed. Many may have survived if there had been enough lifeboats onboard for all the passengers.

In 1912, the Titanic was the largest ship ever to be built. Many people thought it was unsinkable.

JAPAN AIRLINES FLIGHT 123

The crash of Japan Airlines Flight 123 is the worst crash in history to involve just one plane. A poor repair job after an earlier minor accident caused Flight 123 to crash over Japan in 1985. Just four people survived, and 520 people were killed in the crash.

DOÑA PAZ

The *Doña Paz*, seen here three years before it sank, was designed to carry about 1,500 people. Many more were on the ferry when it sank, though.

DOÑA PAZ

The *Doña Paz* was a ferry boat used to carry people from one place to another in the Philippines. While traveling to Manila on December 20, 1987, the *Doña Paz* struck the *Vector*, an oil tanker. A fire spread across the two ships and about 4,000 people were killed.

23

TERRORISM: USING VIOLENCE AND FEAR

Many people want to change the way governments and people think and act. Many use civil and peaceful methods, such as voting in elections and protesting laws. However, some people try to use violence and fear to control others. This is called **terrorism**. Acts of terrorism can range from bombings and plane crashes to violent attacks and murder.

In April 2013, terrorists used bombs to kill three people and injure hundreds in Boston. Terrorist attacks in the United States are rare, though. Members of the government, as well as police and firefighters, work hard to prevent terrorist acts before they happen.

The twin towers were struck by airplanes at 8:46 am and 9:03 am. Less than two hours later, both buildings had collapsed.

Many buildings around the twin towers were damaged by fire and falling debris.

9/11

On September 11, 2001, two planes were hijacked by terrorists and crashed into the twin towers of the World Trade Center, in New York City. A third plane was crashed into the Pentagon, in Washington, D.C., and a fourth plane crashed in a field in Pennsylvania. By day's end, nearly 3,000 people were dead.

Beslan is a town in Russia. In September 2004, a group of terrorists took over 1,100 people **hostage** at a Beslan school. Many of the hostages were children. When the school was freed three days later, nearly 400 people had been killed.

This photo shows just some of the hostages killed in Beslan.

On December 21, 1988, a bomb exploded on Pan Am Flight 10 as the airplane was on its way from London to New York. The plane crashed in Lockerbie, Scotland, and 270 people were killed. Years later, a terrorist from Libya was found guilty of the bombing.

MAN-MADE DISASTERS AROUND THE WORLD

1. Union Carbide Gas Leak—Bhopal, India

2. London Smog—London, England

3. *Doña Paz*—between Leyte island and Manila, Philippines

4. September 11 Attacks—NYC, Washington, D.C., and Pennsylvania

5. Chernobyl Nuclear Accident—Pripyat, Ukraine

6. *Deepwater Horizon* Oil Spill—Gulf of Mexico

7. Bangladesh Factory Collapse—Savar, Bangladesh

8. Tenerife Airport Disaster—Tenerife island, Spain

9. *Exxon Valdez* Oil Spill—Prince William Sound, Alaska

10. Love Canal—Niagara Falls, New York

11. Donora Smog—Donora, Pennsylvania

12. Picher Lead Contamination—Picher, Oklahoma

DEADLIEST MAN-MADE DISASTERS

Here is a list of the deadliest man-made disasters in history. Some of these disasters were very deadly to humans. Others killed plants, animals, and destroyed parts of the environment. You will find descriptions of many of these disasters in the pages of this book. You can read more about the other events on the list in books, newspaper articles, and on the Internet.

DEADLIEST MAN-MADE

NAME	DATE
Union Carbide Gas Leak	December 2, 1984
London Smog	December 5–9, 1952
Doña Paz	December 20, 1987
September 11 Attacks	September 11, 2001
Chernobyl Nuclear Accident	April 26, 1986
Deepwater Horizon Oil Spill	April 20, 2010
Titanic	April 15, 1912
Bangladesh Factory Collapse	April 24, 2013
Tenerife Airport Disaster	March 27, 1977
Exxon Valdez Oil Spill	March 24, 1989

The world's worst industrial disaster occurred in Bhopal, India, on the night of December 2, 1984. Deadly gas from the Union Carbide pesticide plant leaked into the air from a faulty storage tank. At least 3,787 people died immediately, and hundreds of thousands became sick.

DISASTERS

LOCATION	DEATHS/DAMAGE
Bhopal, India	3,787 immediate, 1,600+ in aftermath
London, England	4,000–12,000
Philippines	4,000+
New York, Washington D.C., Pennsylvania	2,997+
Ukraine	31+ deaths, high rates of cancer
Gulf of Mexico	major damage to marine life
Atlantic Ocean	1,502
Savar, Bangladesh	1,127
Tenerife, Spain	583
Prince William Sound, Alaska	major damage to marine life

Note—It is not always possible to know the exact number of people killed in a man-made disaster. Sometimes people are considered missing, and the bodies of victims are simply never found. In this book, we have made every effort to use the most reliable numbers available.

LEARNING FROM OUR MISTAKES

Man-made disasters are caused by the actions of people. For that reason, we, as people, control whether we create more disasters like the ones in this book or choose to learn from our mistakes. Many of the events you have read about could have been prevented if people understood the danger of their actions. By understanding what caused these disasters, we will better know how to stop events like this from happening in the future!

Around the world, soldiers train in different situations with the goal of preventing terrorist attacks from occurring.

GLOSSARY

chemicals (KEH-mih-kulz) Matter that can be mixed with other matter to cause changes.

climate change (KLY-mut CHAYNJ) Changes in Earth's weather that were caused by things people did.

contaminate (kun-TA-mih-nayt) The state of being made unfit for use.

fossil fuel (FAH-sul FYOOL) Fuels, such as coal, natural gas, or gasoline, that were made from plants that died millions of years ago.

hostage (HOS-tij) A person held as a prisoner until some condition is agreed to.

industrial (in-DUS-tree-ul) Having to do with systems of work.

petroleum (peh-TROH-lee-um) An oily liquid that can be used to make gasoline and other products.

pollution (puh-LOO-shun) Man-made wastes that harm Earth's air, land, or water.

radiation (ray-dee-AY-shun) Rays of light, heat, or energy that spread outward from something.

reactors (ree-AK-turz) Places in which nuclear reactions are carried out.

smog (SMOG) Pollution in the air.

terrorism (TER-ur-iz-um) The system of using violence or fear to control people.

toxic waste (TOK-sik WAYST) Waste products, often made by manufacturing, that make the land dirty and can be poisonous.

INDEX

WEBSITES

Due to the changing nature of Internet links, PowerKids Press has developed an online list of websites related to the subject of this book. This site is updated regularly. Please use this link to access the list: www.powerkids.com/twd/man/